Banquet & Ashes

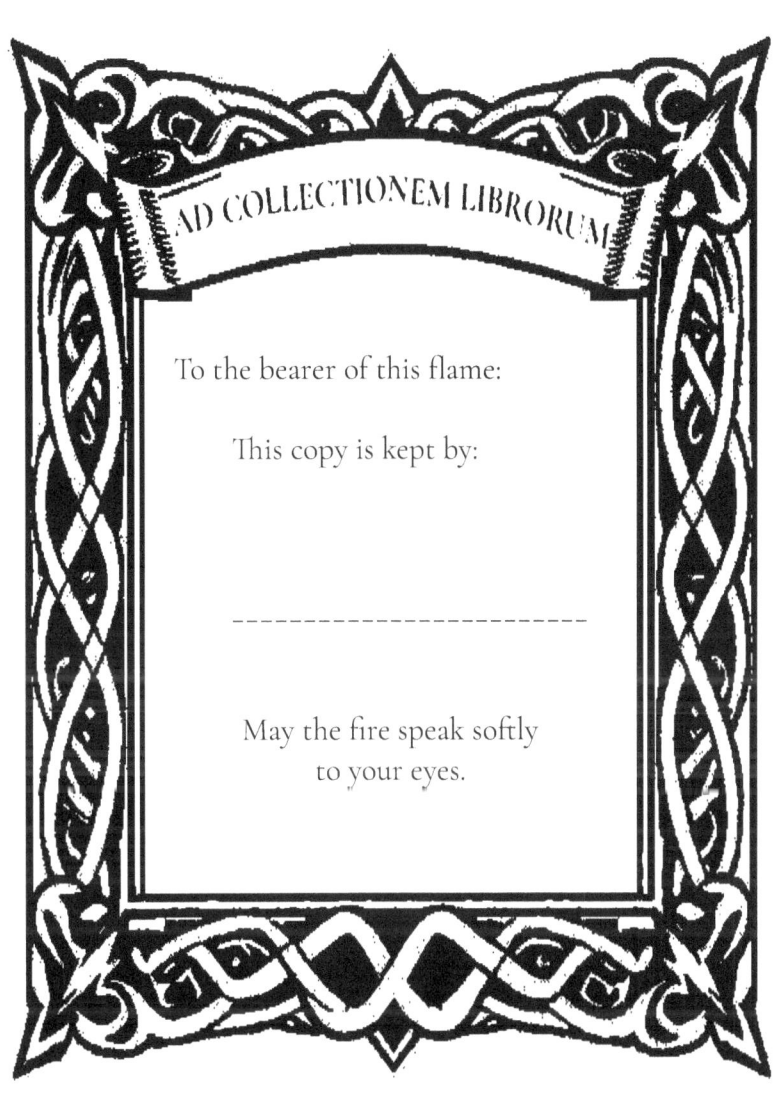

AD COLLECTIONEM LIBRORUM

To the bearer of this flame:

This copy is kept by:

_____

May the fire speak softly
to your eyes.

Edited by Jordan River
Cover Art © 2025 by Lou-Ellen Allwood
Internal Calligraphy illustrations original work © 2025 Jordan River
Spiritus Ignis, p. 12 © 2025 by Jordan River
Typeset in Cormorant Garamond and IM Fell
Printed and bound in the US by IngramSpark
Published by Little Loom Press

Library of Congress Control Number: Pending
ISBN: 979-8-9928666-2-9 1st Hardcover Gift Edition
ISBN: 979-8-9928666-0-5 **1st Printing Paperback**
ISBN: 979-8-9928666-1-2 1st Printing E-book

Banquet & Ashes

A Book of Gold & Hunger, of Gates & Fire,
of Feasts That Devour and Flames That Purge

Inscribed by Jordan River, Witness

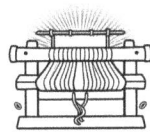

ISBN: 979-8-9928666-0-5
Publisher: Little Loom Press
@ 2025 by Jordan River. All rights reserved.
Softcover 1st Printing 4/2025

Dedicated
to those who keep striving—despite the evidence;
to those who help—we need you;
to those left behind—we see you;
to the top—heed the warnings or the fire awaits.

Acknowledgments
Mr Psolka and Sylvia. Two fantastic English teachers from a different era.
Dante, Milton, and Jonathon Edwards. For their fire.
My cover artist and designer Lou-Ellen. Thank you!
All who came before and all who come after.
My Muse.

Contents

Foreword

There are those who feast, and those who watch.
There are those who climb, and those who never arrive.

There are gates that stand fast, glass that will never break,
tables that groan beneath their burden.

There are voices—soft with ease, loud with hunger, distant with
judgment.

There are crowns that gleam but never change hands,
hands that toil but never hold power,
power that fattens itself until it becomes grotesque.

And there is always, **always** a reckoning.

Across golden halls and mirrored walls,
between the hush of wealth and the roar of longing,
the feast endures.

It is ancient, ceaseless, inevitable—
and it is **never** for you.

But there is another truth, one they do not speak:
Not all are seated.
Not all accept The Feast.

Beyond the gilded halls, hands pass bread without payment.

Beyond the banquet's glare, fire is kindled for warmth, not ruin.

Beyond the gates, there are those who build,
who plant,
who make anew.

This book is not a revolution, nor a sermon, nor a simple lament.

It is a reckoning in measured steps—
a descent through golden halls and empty promises,
through revelry that turns to rot,
through hunger that is never sated.

It is a map of inevitability,
guiding us from the locked gate to the Feast that devours itself,
from the climb that leads nowhere
to the moment where fire is the only answer.

Here you will find no heroes, no saviors—
only what is,
what has always been,
and what will always return.

For as long as there are those who hoard,
there will be those who hunger.
And as long as there is hunger,
there will be a banquet.

A banquet of gold,
of flesh,
of excess—
and, at last, a banquet of ashes.

This book is its own gate.

Open it.

Step through.

Let The Feast begin.

Beyond the high hedge, laughter spills like wine. Light pools on marble, drowning distant shadows. The bell pull hangs, untarnished, never worn by touch of stranger's hand.

The Gilded Gate

The golden world is quiet, walled and high,
Its gardens bright, its voices soft with ease.
The old names whisper—low, refined, and dry,
While others claw for scraps their lords release.

The lucky climb, but none may claim the throne.
Their gold still reeks of sweat, their hands too rough.
The gates admit no names but those well-known;
For new crowns shine, but never shine enough.

And those below? They toil and dream and drown,
Their hands outstretched to those who do not see.
They press against the glass—they cry, they pound,
Yet beggars' hands shall never find the key.

The gate is strong; the lock will never rust.
The world outside may burn—it will not bust.

The marble gleams too bright, its veins spreading like cracks. Champagne bubbles rise and burst, while beneath the parquet floor, timbers whisper and shift.

A Sharper Warning

Gold is heavy; it bends the bough.
Too much weight—ye hear it now?
The latch still holds, the lock still stays,
But wood will splinter, stone will fray.

The feast is long, the wine still sweet,
No hollow ring of marching feet.
No fire upon the windless air—
But do ye think none gather there?

Gold is heavy; it sinks, it drags,
The tide still rises, fills the crags.
Ye weigh it down, ye press it deep—
The dam will hold—until it weeps.

In mirrored halls, every candle flame becomes a constellation. Perfume hangs thick as promises, while orchestral notes spiral endlessly through gilt and glass. Behind each smile, muscles strain to hold the proper shape

The Masquerade

Gold leaf laughter, veiled delight,
Dance and drink and drown the night.
Glasses high, the toasts grow bold—
Clink and shimmer, gods of gold.

Guilt is cheap, and grace is gone,
What's a sin beneath the song?
Turn ye not, nor glance behind—
Who recalls the debts they signed?

Glitter bright, the curtains drawn,
Perfumed hands pass pearls at dawn.
Step ye light, the floor is sound—
And none, they say, have ever drowned.

The air thins here, at the edge of promise. Light falls strange on polished surfaces, creating mirrors that lead nowhere. Every doorway echoes with departing footsteps, yet the halls remain empty.

The Climb That Never Comes

Step and strive, but mind the floor,
The gates stand fast, the glass is high.
Ye climb, but reach the door no more.

They raise their cups, they call for more,
Old names still shine, they never die.
Step and strive, but mind the floor.

Gold may gleam, but not restore,
A borrowed name, a borrowed sky.
Ye climb, but reach the door no more.

Turn ye not to beg or implore,
A knock unanswered, no reply.
Step and strive, but mind the floor.

Some may fall, some wash ashore,
Some fade, some rise, some wonder why—
Ye climb, but reach the door no more.

The gates stand fast, the glass is high.
Step and strive, but mind the floor.

Midword

The silver is polished.
The knives are sharpened.
The seats are full.

The table does not move.
But it remembers.

It knows the weight of every body that has sat before.
It knows the hands that have gripped its edge, trembling.
It knows the scent
of hunger,
of indulgence,
of fear.

They speak of lineage, of legacy, of law.
They do not speak of the ones beneath them.
They do not ask who carved the roast.
They do not ask who poured the wine.

They do not see the reflection beneath the glass.

But the table groans.
And it remembers.

They drink deep.
The wine does not empty.
They carve and tear.
The bones do not break.

They lean closer—
laughing,
ravenous,
radiant.

And in the gleam of the candlelight,

The Feast looks back.

A hundred hands reaching.
A hundred mouths open.
A hundred faces, the same as their own.

They do not stop eating.
They cannot stop eating.
Because if they do they will have to see.

The table does not laugh.
The table does not sigh.

The table simply waits.

The feast does not end.
But some will rise.
The fire does not cleanse those who have already left.
And before them, on the table—

the feast devours itself.

Not all stand in the hall, waiting for a seat.
Below—
Candlelight gilds the dishes, endless as stars.
The servants' hands blur with motion,
bearing away untasted delicacies,
bringing fresh sacrifices to the altar of appetite.

In the kitchen, garbage gathers in golden hills.

The Vile Banquet

Behold the feast of gilded sin,
Where tables groan beneath the din
Of corpulence made flesh anew,
The wine as red as the debt past due.

Here sits the lord with rings of gold,
His hands too fat for truths untold.
The lady swathed in silken lies,
Her pearls are strung with others' cries.

The bread is baked of withered grain,
Harvested from the land in pain.
The fruits, once bright, are bruised and sour,
Plucked by hands long crushed for power.

A roasted beast, its bones exposed,
Its eyes are glass, its ribs foreclosed.
It turns upon a spit of gold,
Its flesh is rank, its fat grown cold.

Eat, my lords, my ladies fair,
Your feast is set; your sins laid bare.
The silver shines, the glasses clink,
You eat; the poor have naught but stink.

So feast, oh kings of vacant halls,
And gorge upon the fruit that falls.
Your laughter echoes, hollow, thin—
For gluttony shall eat within.

Yet every bite shall choke thee now,
The meat is ash; the wine's a vow—
A curse upon your glutted pride,
For all you've stolen, all you've lied.

And as the candles sputter low,
Your shadows stretch, your corpulence grows.
The banquet fades, the plates are bare,
Still hunger lingers in the air.

You'll eat again, and ever more,
Yet never leave this wretched door.
For wealth is fat, and greed the chain—
Eat now, my lords, and eat thy pain.

Spiritus Ignis

Fire speaks in tongues of gold and crimson, consuming pretense first, then substance. In its wake, ash settles like fresh snow, and the air tastes of beginning.

The Cleansing Ember

Let fire take the feast of sin,
Burn clean the fat, the rot within.
May golden rings be turned to dust,
And pearls dissolve, unstrung by trust.

The bread shall rise in honest hands,
The grain reclaimed by kinder lands.
Let fruits grow sweet from soil made new,
No longer bruised by what they knew.

The beast once bound shall turn to bone,
Its spirit free, its suffering flown.
The wine, once blood, now runs so clear,
No bitter vow, no taste of fear.

Let hands once clasped in want now weave,
Not grasp for gold, nor hoard, nor thieve.
Let tables stand where none are lord,
And none go silent, none ignored.

Let ember's tongue unmake deceit,
Turn ash to soil beneath our feet.
Where once the table towered tall,
Let open hands rebuild for all.

Let silence fall where lies were sown,
Where hollow feasts once claimed the throne.
Let truth take root where hunger swayed,
And debts be met, long left unpaid.

So break the table, crack the throne,
Let wealth be weight, not tethered stone.
No hunger now, no gilded chain—
Let greed dissolve like autumn rain.

Yet mark this well, you lords of vice:
To feast again, pay thrice the price.
For should you hoard, should falsehood thrive,
The banquet wakes—it will arrive.

And should ye forge the chains anew,
Or raise the glass to power's due,
The fire waits—it does not die.
It only sleeps. It will reply.

Afterword

I have dwelt in absences—
in the space between mirror and reflection,
in the silence after laughter fades,
in the moment between reaching and grasping.

I saw the gates close,
the gold glisten,
the laughter rise and fade.

I watched them feast as if tomorrow would never come,
as if abundance could outweigh consequence.

When the fire came, I did not need to stay—

I knew how the marble would weep,
how the crystal would shatter,
how ash would taste of beginning.

They will build new tables.
They will forge new locks.

They will pour wine and raise glasses and believe themselves...
immune...

to time.
to history.
to **consequence**.

But no one is safe once the table is set.

Feaster or feasted upon—all will be consumed.

Their hands, once so heavy with gold,
will grasp at nothing.

Their names, once spoken in reverence,
will fall to dust.

Their laughter will echo—
but only in hunger's hollow gut.

And I will be there,
in the shadows their mirrors cannot catch,
in the spaces their unseeing creates.

The Feast always returns.

The hunger never learns.

From shadow to shadow, I remember and remain.

Watching.

Waiting.

Knowing it begins again.

Endnotes

The Ashes Still Speak
The Feast thrives on silence.
Speak, and you become its enemy.

Fire cleanses. Fire forgets.
Which do you believe?

They will feast again. And they will call it new.
If you think The Feast does not concern you, look again.
You sit at their table, or you lie on it.
(whispered: "Was the table ever whole?")

The strong write the laws. The dead write the lessons.
The wise write them anew.
The fire does not ask who built the table—
but you should.
They will call it fate.
You will know it was choice.
(whispered: "There is no clean wealth. Only unexamined wealth.")

The Feast is Not Inevitable
A full table does not mean a fair table.
Power justifies. Justice remembers.

To suffer is not to be good. To prosper is not to be right.
There is no sin in need. There is no virtue in greed.
(whispered: "The table is set before the guests arrive.")

Excess is sin. Hoarding is vice.
To watch suffering and not intervene is to condone cruelty.
The trials of one are the trials of us all.
(whispered: "Life is struggle. Be kind.")

The Table can be broken. The Feast delayed.
The hunger of those who consume is checked by your will.

You cannot be both guest and witness.
To accept a seat is to accept the rules.
(whispered: "If The Feast always returns, then so must the ones who refuse or remake it.")

Revolutions are not won at the banquet.
They begin in the kitchen.

Choose.

There Are Other Ways
Fire is not the only answer.
A broken table can be mended.
A broken hearth can be tended.

Not all revolutions burn.
Some plant, some build, some teach.
(whispered: "A feast shared is a Feast undone.")

The only wealth that endures is the kind that moves.
You do not have to sit at their table.
There are other halls, other hands, other ways.
(whispered: "If the table is set before the guests arrive, then change the hands that set it.")

You are not the first to see.

You are not the first to turn away.

Those who left the table are waiting.

Find them.

Footnotes

The Ash That Settles After the Fire

A banquet ended, but not for the first time. The air is thick with what was. The table is cold, but still waiting. Listen—do you hear them?

They believed The Feast would last forever.

They were wrong.

Rome, 476 CE:
They dined as the Goths broke the gates.
Silver goblets raised high—toast to the Empire.
By dawn, the city belonged to another.

A kingdom is never lost in a day. It is only claimed.

By the end of 476, the last Roman emperor, Romulus Augustulus, had abdicated. The empire did not fall in fire, but in bureaucracy and betrayal.

France, 1789:
The bread was too thin; the tables too full.
Marie did not say 'cake,' but the streets burned just the same.
And the guillotine did not stop at kings.

Justice is not always kind. It is only fair.

By 1793, the monarchy was dead. By 1799, so was the Republic that killed it.

Weimar, 1929-1933
They drank deep as the market gasped.
Berlin glittered—cabaret, champagne, skin and silk.
The republic swayed, and the bankers held their breath.
Then came the crash.
Then came the fire.
Then came the knife.

A Feast in crisis is not a feast. It is an auction.

By 1930, the Reichstag was paralyzed. By 1932, the streets were battlegrounds. By 1933, democracy was a formality.

Wealth had made its choice.

They set the table again.
They always do.

But history does not dine—
it only watches,
waiting for the moment the Feast begins to rot.

America, Present Day:
The Feast continues.
The halls shine bright.
The doors are locked.

The wealth gap widens, the stock market soars—
the hunger lines stretch.

They set the table again. And they call it new.

-Iterum-

Jordan River writes at the crossroads of history, power, and reckoning, crafting poetry that unearths the weight of excess and the cost of hunger. A former researcher and hobbyist linguist, Jordan's work draws on the rhythms of prophecy, the echoes of lost voices, and the inevitability of collapse. With a keen ear for cadence and contradiction, their poetry explores the gilded illusions of wealth, the specters of the forgotten, and the fire that follows feast.

When not writing, Jordan can be found tracing the fault lines of history, wandering through abandoned places, or listening for the whispers of what comes next.

The table is set. The question remains.

Benedictus Cineris
You held the fire.
It did not consume you.
Only revealed you.
Let the ashes speak.

www.ingramcontent.com/pod-product-compliance
Lightning Source LLC
Chambersburg PA
CBHW051604120626
46551CB00013B/1659